Contents 1A

Note to the teacher

The National Curriculum

The 37 songs in Key Stage 1 address all the relevant programmes of study. They take account of children's vocal development with particular reference to increasing children's pitch range, to extending children's memory, and to performing from and understanding notational and musical instructions. They introduce children to an extensive repertoire which addresses issues of stylistic and cultural variety. They include songs chosen for dramatization, movement, counting and language development. The notes attached to each song indicate the ways in which they can be used and developed, and the aspects of the scheme that they support.

Guitar chords have been suggested for all the songs. The guitar is a more appropriate and intimate instrument to use with young voices. If this is not possible then it would be better to sing the songs unaccompanied.

Percussion accompaniment has also been suggested. It must be appreciated that accompanying a song is a very sophisticated activity.

It is not anticipated that the songs will necessarily be introduced in the order in which they stand. Teaching circumstances vary so much that teachers should select and use the songs in a way most appropriate to their own classroom situations. For general guidance a brief note is included in the contents list to indicate the potential of each song.

Recommended songbooks

Apusskidu	
Okki-tokki-unga	A & C Black
Game-Songs with Prof Dogg's Troupe	
Sing-a-Song One	Thomas Nelson & Sons Ltd.
Sing-a-Song Two	
Knock at the Door	Ward Lock Educational
This Little Puffin	Puffin Books
Festivals	Oxford University Press

Nice to have books

Singing Fun   George G. Harrap & Co. Ltd.
The Clarendon Books of Singing Games (Books 1 and 2)   Oxford University Press

Ten Galloping Horses   Frederick Warne Ltd.
Jumping, Laughing, Resting: Songs for a New Generation   Oak Publications
This Funny Family   Ward Lock Educational
Harlequin
Count me in   A & C Black
Jump into the ring   Ward Lock Educational

Counting songs

Forwards

One little elephant went out to play   *Okki-tokki-unga*
Peter works with one hammer   *This Little Puffin*
Johnny taps with one hammer   *Okki-tokki-unga*

John Brown had a little Indian   *This Little Puffin*
One man went to mow   *This Little Puffin*
This old man   *Okki-tokki-unga*
The ants go marching   *Okki-tokki-unga*
Ten little chickens (forward and back in twos)   *Sing-a-Song One*
Hickety Tickety   *Sing-a-Song One*
The animals went in two by two   *Apusskidu*
One little brown bird   *Oxford Primary Music Stage 1A*

Backwards

Ten green bottles hanging on the wall   *Traditional*
Five little ducks went swimming one day   *This Little Puffin*
Five currant buns in a baker's shop   *This Little Puffin*
Five little speckled frogs   *Apusskidu, Sing-a-Song Two*
Ten in a bed   *Apusskidu*
Five little firemen   *Sing-a-Song One*
Ten fat sausages sizzling in the pan (counting in twos)   *Okki-tokki-unga*
Ten little squirrels sat on a tree   *Okki-tokki-unga*
Ten miles from home   *Singing Fun*
Six little frogs (counting in twos)   *Knock at the Door*
Ten little men   *Sing-a-Song One*
Three astronauts   *Sing-a-Song Two*

NOTE *Ten Galloping Horses* has a section on number rhyme songs.
This Little Puffin also has a section on number songs and rhymes.

Some useful songs

The following songs underline the musical concepts introduced in Stage 1A. They can all be found in the recommended songbooks.

Loud/Quiet

I'm a dingle dangle scarecrow   *This Little Puffin, Sing-a-Song One*
Oh we can play on the big bass drum   *Okki-tokki-unga*

Join in the game   *Okki-tokki-unga*
Miss Polly had a dolly   *Okki-tokki-unga, This Little Puffin*
The oak tree   *Sing-a-Song One*

(Sing the first two verses quietly to indicate the size of the tiny seed; then louder on the last verse as you sing about the 'great big spreading oak tree'.)
Many songs can be sung *loudly* at first and repeated *quietly*.

Quick/Slow

Slowly and quickly (poem)   *Sing-a-Song One*
Good morning Mister Wind   *Knock at the Door*
Mary is a doctor (make up more verses involving different speeds)   *Knock at the Door*
Wiggley Woo (make up more verses involving speeds of different animals)   *Sing-a-Song One*
Slowly, slowly walks my Grandad   *This Little Puffin*
The wheels on the bus   *This Little Puffin, Knock at the Door*

Many songs can be sung *quickly* at first and then repeated *slowly*.

Different speeds and ways of moving

Games to play with feet (all the songs in this section are excellent for this purpose)   *This Little Puffin*
A thin man walked along   *This Little Puffin*
Mister Jumping Jack   *This Little Puffin*
As I was walking down the street   *This Little Puffin*
Can you walk on two legs   *This Little Puffin*
Clapping and
We'll all go a-walking   *Sing-a-Song Two*
The ants go marching   *Okki-tokki-unga*
The grand old duke of York   *Okki-tokki-unga*
The guard song   *Apusskidu*
The elephant   *Apusskidu*
The circus   *Sing-a-Song One*

How did Jane come to school?

Words and music by Leonora Davies

Brightly

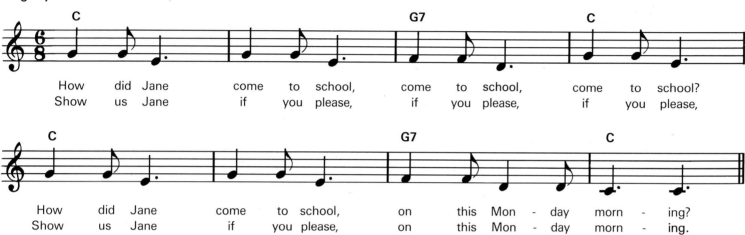

How did Jane come to school, come to school, come to school?
Show us Jane if you please, if you please, if you please,

How did Jane come to school, on this Mon - day morn - ing?
Show us Jane if you please, on this Mon - day morn - ing.

Singing game

Choose one child to go into the centre of the circle. Everyone dances round singing the first part of the song. The singing then stops whilst 'Jane' shows the class how she came to school. The rest of the children join in with her movements quite freely. Jane chooses another child to take her place in the centre and rejoins the circle. The song continues.

Follow up

Talk about the sounds of the children's feet as they come to school, focusing upon the rhythms of the various movements. Use this as a theme for a movement session: ask the children to respond to different rhythms played on a drum or tambour, and sequence a number of rhythms that might represent a typical coming to school journey. Finally, let the children work out in movement their own journey — unaccompanied.

Musical ideas

These will relate to the children's movement. Is it quick or slow? Do the children walk, run or skip?

Related songs and movement activities

The section 'Games to play with feet' in *This Little Puffin* has many excellent songs that will act as a stimulus to extend the follow up suggestions. See also the song 'Slowly, slowly walks my Grandad'.

Refer back to Pupils' Book 1A pages 4 and 5 relating them to the song. What *sounds* do the children hear on their way to school?

Come and dance with me

Words and music by Jean Gilbert

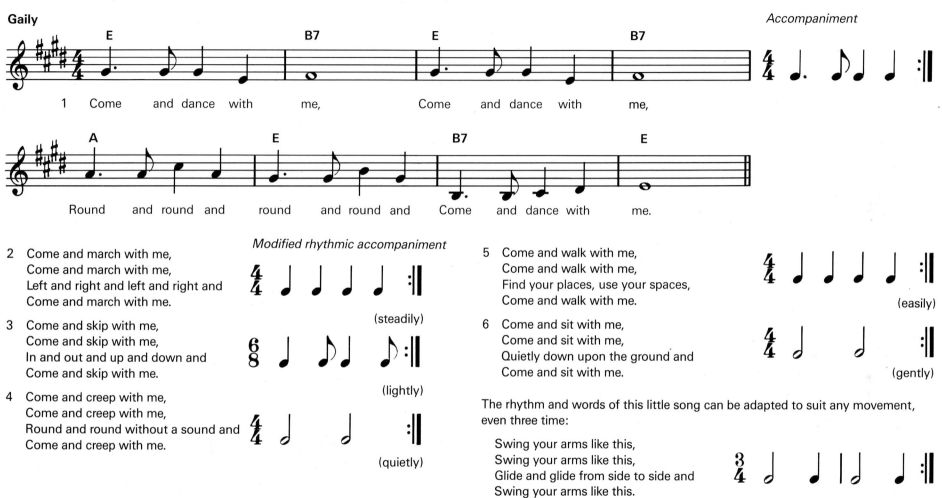

Gaily

Accompaniment

1 Come and dance with me, Come and dance with me,

Round and round and round and round and Come and dance with me.

2 Come and march with me,
Come and march with me,
Left and right and left and right and
Come and march with me.

Modified rhythmic accompaniment

(steadily)

3 Come and skip with me,
Come and skip with me,
In and out and up and down and
Come and skip with me.

(lightly)

4 Come and creep with me,
Come and creep with me,
Round and round without a sound and
Come and creep with me.

(quietly)

5 Come and walk with me,
Come and walk with me,
Find your places, use your spaces,
Come and walk with me.

(easily)

6 Come and sit with me,
Come and sit with me,
Quietly down upon the ground and
Come and sit with me.

(gently)

The rhythm and words of this little song can be adapted to suit any movement, even three time:

Swing your arms like this,
Swing your arms like this,
Glide and glide from side to side and
Swing your arms like this.

Musical ideas

A wide variety of concepts and musical ideas can be introduced through move-ment: different rhythms, speeds and dynamics — loud and quiet. In this case it will depend upon how the basic rhythm of the song is modified to suit the various verses. A tambourine is a good instrument to underline the rhythm; it is versatile too and can be adapted to accompany all the verses.

Extending the song

Introduce each verse or different movement by playing the *rhythm* first. The children must guess what kind of movement they can do to that rhythm. Perhaps they can make up their own words to fit their movement.

Dance in a circle

Louisiana French folk song

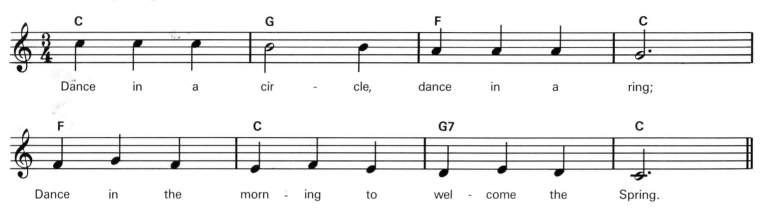

Dance in a circle, dance in a ring;

Dance in the morning to welcome the Spring.

Here is another quite different song that can be adapted in the same way for movement:

Dance on your own
Around and around;
Dance very slowly
Now sit on the ground.

March, skip, walk, creep and so on.

Our instrument song

Traditional tune, words by Jean Gilbert

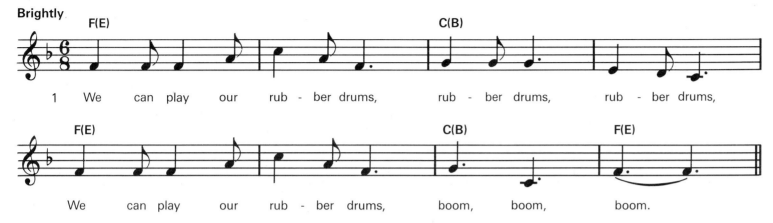

2 We can play our castanets ...... *click, click, click*

3 We can play our tambourines .... *tap, tap, tap*

4 We can play our jingle bells ..... *chink, chink, chink*

5 We can play our shakers .... *shake, shake, shake*

6 We can play our triangles .... *ting, ting, ting*

7 We can play our instruments .... *la, la, la.*

Comments

This is a good song to use when introducing simple percussion instruments and will help the children learn to handle the instruments and control their playing. It can complement the children's experience of using sound makers in the music corner, but wait until the children are fairly familiar with them before introducing the song itself. Start with one or two verses only and gradually build up. Adapt the words to suit your own instruments. Aim for rhythmic playing and accept the children's own beats. They will soon join in the singing as the tune is well known.

Musical ideas

Each verse can be sung in a different way to illustrate the musical concepts that are being introduced at this stage.

> e.g. Loudly play our rubber drums . . . (bongo drums)
> Quietly play our rubber drums . . .
> Quickly play our rubber drums . . .
> Slowly play our rubber drums . . .

Follow up

Leave some of the quieter instruments in the music corner and prepare cards for the relevant verses:

Quietly play our jingle bells	Loudly play our jingle bells

Encourage the children to play the rhythm of the verse they have chosen in the appropriate way. This activity also includes reading experience. With a non-reading group the use of colours for the words 'quietly' 'loudly' 'quickly' 'slowly' might help.

Further songs

What shall we do now it's Autumn time   *Sing-a-Song One*
The band   *This Little Puffin* and *Okki-tokki-unga*
Aiken drum   (adapted for instruments)   *Sing-a-Song One*

I can hear two soldiers

Words and music by Leonora Davies

In march time

Comments

This is a good song to use with instruments once you have introduced them to the children in percussion groups as outlined on page 7. The children should be acquiring a self discipline, which is necessary if activities involving instruments are going to be productive. Keep a steady pulse going with a drum to encourage the children to play and march in time.

Musical ideas

Getting louder — getting quieter. Can the children say what happens to the sound when more soldiers join in, then march away?

Ostinato

The following tune can be played as a repeating pattern on the chime bars or xylophone. It will also help to keep the pulse going:

Singing game

Use a variety of instruments. The children sit in a circle with an instrument placed on the floor in front of them. Choose two children to play their instruments while everyone sings. At each singing two more children join in, thus swelling the sound of the soldiers:

I can hear four soldiers . . .
I can hear six soldiers . . .

Finally all the children will be playing. There are then two ways of ending the song:

1 the children stop playing and count backwards as the verses proceed
2 the playing gets quieter and quieter as the soldiers march away:
    I can hear the soldiers
    Marching far away.
    Left, right, left, right,
    Marching far away.

Continue humming and play *very, very* quietly.

If classroom conditions are suitable, the children can sing, play and march round the room.

The children can also play the game counting forwards and backwards in threes and fours if you adapt the words.

8

Ten little pennies

Traditional tune, words by Jean Gilbert

Clearly

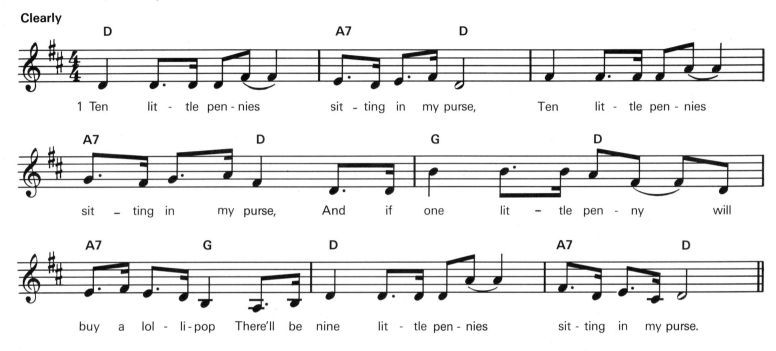

2   Nine little pennies sitting in my purse . . .
    And if one little penny will buy a liquorice . . . (or lollipop again)

Counting back in twos

Ten little pennies sitting in my purse . . .
And if two little pennies will buy a cherry cake . . .

Counting back in fives

Ten little pennies sitting in my purse . . .
And if five little pennies will buy a counting book . . .

Counting back in threes or fours

Start with twelve pennies and adapt as before.

Comments

This is a good example of how to write your own song using a well known tune — in this case 'Ten green bottles'. This particular song could easily be used in connection with some number work or shop project. It has numerous possibilities. Use real objects to count with and number flash cards to support each verse.

What can we hear when we all wake up?

Words and music by Jean Gilbert

Brightly

CHORUS
What can we hear when we all wake up, all wake up, all wake up?

What can we hear when we all wake up, when we all wake up in the morn - ing?

VERSE
1 We can hear the milk - man come, milk - man come, milk - man come.

We can hear the milk - man come, when we all wake up in the morn - ing.

Suggested percussion

cymbals or carefully rattle milk bottles together

2 We can hear the postman come . . .   clappers

3 We can hear the alarm clock . . .   triangle

4 We can hear the kitten meow . . .
   When she wants to come in/go out in the morning voices

Comments and musical ideas

This song focuses on environmental sounds. It is also a good example of the question and answer form which will link with language work. Do choose verses that reflect what the children in your group actually hear — better still get them to make them up.

Just sing and mime the actions to begin with. Later on add percussion. Use this song to discuss which morning sounds are *loud* and which ones are *quiet*.

Musical game

Use the instruments that the children have already chosen to accompany their song. Put these behind a screen or table. Sing the chorus and then play *one* of these instruments. The children should be able to sing the appropriate verse.

10

The little pig

Texan folk song

Not too fast

2   Now that little pig curled up in a heap,
    Oink, oink, oink,   shakers
  Now that little pig curled up in a heap,
  He joined his friends and they went to sleep,
    Oink, oink, oink.

3   They slept and slept and slept and slept,   sand block
    Mm, mm, mm,
  They slept and slept and slept and slept
  And slept and slept and slept and slept —
    Mm, mm, mm.

4   The farmer woke them one by one,   clappers
    Oink, oink, oink,
  The farmer woke them one by one
  And then they rolled out in the sun,   shakers
    Oink, oink, oink.

Suggested percussion

5   They rolled and rolled and rolled and rolled
    (repeat ad lib)   shakers

6   Those little pigs rolled back in their pen,
    Oink, oink, oink,   shakers
  Those little pigs rolled back in their pen
  And then they went to sleep again,
    Oink. oink, oink.

7   Finish by humming through   sand blocks

This is a nonsense song in the folk idiom. It could be dramatized in the hall when the movement could be accompanied by the suggested percussion.

The farmyard

Words and music by Leonora Davies

Gaily but not too fast

1 One day as I walked round the farm I met a lit - tle cat. The
lit - tle cat she said 'Let's play', I said that I'd like that. Me -
ow me - ow, That makes me ve - ry hap - py Me -
ow, me - ow, That makes me ve - ry glad.

2   One day as I walked round the farm
    I met a nice brown cow.
    The nice brown cow she said 'Let's play',
    I said 'Oh yes right now'.
    Moo-oo, moo-oo, that makes me very happy,
    Moo-oo, moo-oo, that makes me very glad.

3   One day as I walked round the farm,
    I met a gentle horse.
    The gentle horse she said 'Let's play'
    I said 'Oh yes of course'.
    Neigh, neigh, that makes me very happy,
    Neigh, neigh, that makes me very glad.

12

4 One day as I walked round the farm,
  I met a fat brown hen.
  The fat brown hen she said 'Let's play',
  I said 'Will you tell me when?'
  Cluck, cluck, that makes me very happy,
  Cluck, cluck, that makes me very glad.

5 One day as I walked round the farm,
  A tractor drove by me.
  The tractor said 'Do you want a ride?'
  I said 'Oh yes please'.
  Brum brum, that makes me very happy,
  Brum brum, that makes me very glad.

Comments

Sing this song to the children first and invite them to join in with the animal sounds at the end of each verse. Later the verses could be acted out by choosing pairs of children — one to walk round the circle of singers and one to be the appropriate animal. They meet. This will reinforce the pattern of the words. Encourage the children to think of some more farm animals and help them make up their own verses.

Musical ideas

Which animals move *quickly* and which move *slowly*?
Which animals make *loud* sounds and which make *quiet* ones?

Related songs

Old Macdonald had a farm   *Sing-a-Song One*
I went to visit a farm one day   *Sing-a-Song One*
There was a farmer had a dog   *Sing-a-Song Two*
The farmer's in his den   *Sing-a-Song One*

Refer back to Pupils' Book 1A page 7 (In the country). Listen the sounds of the farm animals on the tape.

Colours

Joan Raeside

Jauntily

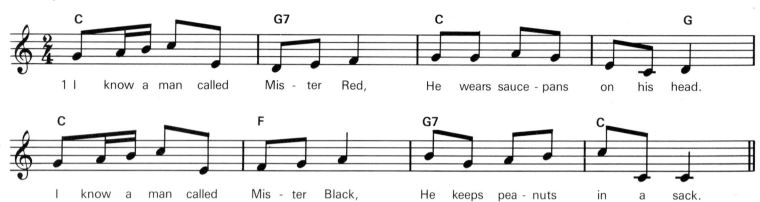

1 I know a man called Mis - ter Red, He wears sauce - pans on his head.

I know a man called Mis - ter Black, He keeps pea - nuts in a sack.

2 I know a man called Mister Pink,
  He fell head first in the sink,
  I know a man called Mister Blue,
  He keeps white mice in his shoe.

3 I know a man called Mister Brown,
  He rides tigers into town,
  I know a man called Mister Green,
  Nicest man I've ever seen.

This is just a fun song! It invites more verses about other colours and any situation
will do so long as there is another rhyming word for the new colour.

Five little field mice

Cynthia Raza

Dramatically

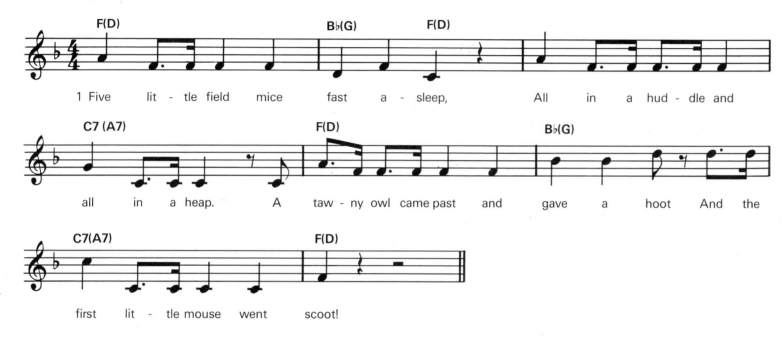

2   Four little field mice fast asleep . . .

3   Three little field mice fast asleep . . .

4   Two little field mice fast asleep . . .

5   One little field mouse fast asleep . . .

6   No little field mice fast asleep . . .

Guitar is easier in D — chords in bracket. Capo up 3 frets.

Singing game

Choose seven children for the field mice, mother mouse and the owl. The rest of the children sing, count and mime all the actions. The owl can tap one of the sleeping mice gently as he 'flies' past each time, and that little mouse can 'scoot' back to mother mouse.

Musical ideas

This song underlines the concepts of *loud* or *quiet* as well as being a useful counting song. Talk to the children about the quietness of night time, and about the shock of loud noises like the owl's hoot, especially when they are unexpected. Encourage them to listen to the night-time sounds outside as they go to bed.

The wind blows east

American

Slow

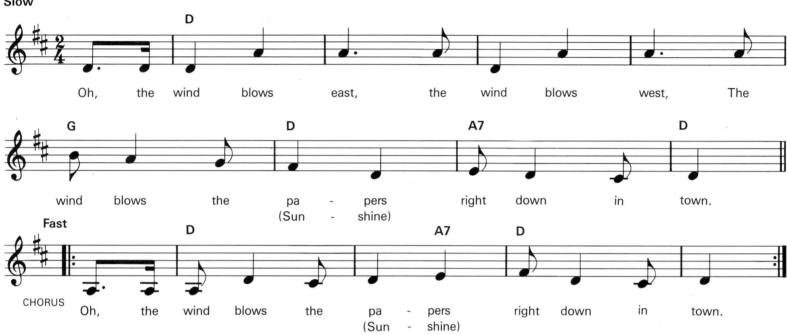

The original word 'Sunshine' used in this song referred to the name of a ship that was blown 'right down in town' during a hurricane in the Bahamas. The original version also uses the word 'blow' instead of 'blows'.

Comments

The children will think of many things that the wind blows 'right down in town', 'right up our street' or 'right through the park': leaves, raindrops, thunder clouds, people's hats, rubbish. It could also blow things 'up in the air' or 'over the wall'. Encourage the children to improvise further verses of their own. Link this song with the sound story *A Windy Day*.

Musical ideas

Sing the first part of the verse very *slowly* so that the children will enjoy the excitement of changing their singing to a really *fast*, lively chorus which can be repeated many times — if you wish, at least four.

Guitar

Guitar can also play in E using chords E A B7 for a slightly higher pitch. An occasional verse sung in this key will add to the variety and excitement of the song.

16

Dancing puppet

Traditional American tune
Words by Jean Gilbert

Steadily; not too fast

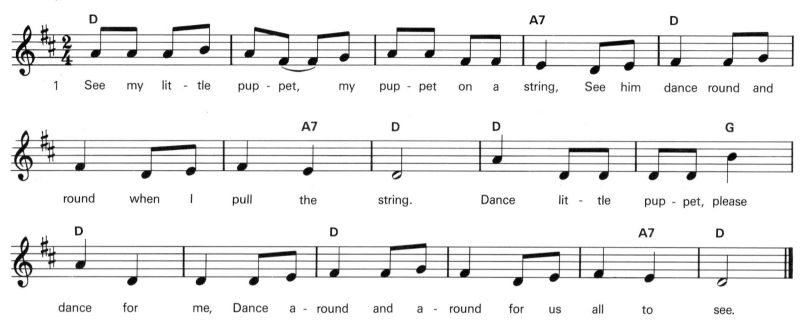

1 See my lit - tle pup - pet, my pup - pet on a string, See him dance round and round when I pull the string. Dance lit - tle pup - pet, please dance for me, Dance a - round and a - round for us all to see.

2 See my little puppet, my puppet on a string,
See him jump up and down when I pull the string.
Jump little puppet, please jump for me,
Jump up and down for us all to see.

3 See my little puppet, my puppet on a string,
See him walk to and fro when I pull the string.
Walk little puppet, please walk for me,
Walk to and fro for us all to see.

4 You can be a puppet, a puppet on a string,
You can dance for me when I pull the string.
Dance round and round, jump up and down,
Do a funny little walk like a funny little clown!

Introduce this song through a suitable toy or puppet or when you have made some simple puppets with the children. Let the children experiment with and describe different kinds of movement they can make with the puppet.

Percussion

Encourage the children to suggest a different percussion instrument for each verse. These can then be put into the music corner together with the puppet. Allow two children at a time to work in this area, one to handle the puppet while the other chooses a suitable instrument to accompany the movement.

Movement

Let the children be puppets controlled by an imaginary string. They can move each part of their bodies in turn, then different parts together and finally make up a puppet dance. Control the movements with a suitable percussion instrument.

Hallowe'en

Words and music by Jean Gilbert

Mysteriously

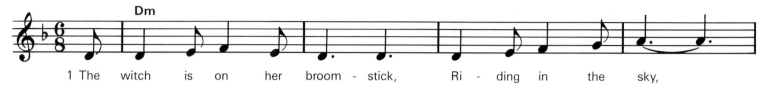

1 The witch is on her broom - stick, Ri - ding in the sky,

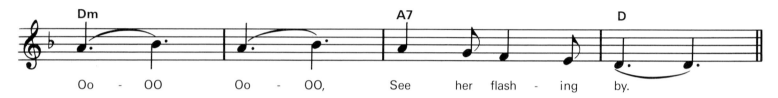

Oo - OO Oo - OO, See her flash - ing by.

2 The wind is howling through the trees,
The sky is very black, (mysteriously)
Oo - oo, oo - oo,
Hallowe'en is back.

3 The cat is prowling through the grass
Can you see her eyes? (quietly)
Meow - meow,
Catch her by surprise! (whisper)

4 The goblins dance and jump about
Up and down the street, (jerkily)
Click clack, click clack,
Go their dancing feet.

Suggested percussion

shakers/sand blocks

tambour with a
padded beater

clappers/castanets

Games

1 Hide the instruments and play them one by one. The children must move and then freeze into a statue of the character represented by the instrument.

2 Let the children work in pairs, one playing, the other moving.

3 Divide the children into as many groups as you have characters and instruments. Each group moves when its own instrument is being played. Occasionally play two or more instruments. The children must watch carefully and listen.

Musical ideas

Each verse introduces a different musical idea. Movement and singing can help the children to absorb these ideas as they respond to the mood of each verse.

Ccomments

This little action song will provide the basis for some dramatic movement. Sing it first in the classroom and encourage the children to make up some more verses about their favourite Hallowe'en characters. Ask them to choose suitable percussion instruments and use these to accompany movement in the hall.

Further Hallowe'en songs

Witch song   *Sing-a-Song One*
There was an old witch   *Sing-a-Song Two*
Witches of Hallowe'en   *Knock at the Door*
Hallowe'en's coming   *Singing Fun*
Hallowe'en is coming   *Sing-a-Song One*

Lullaby

Words and music by Jean Gilbert

Gently

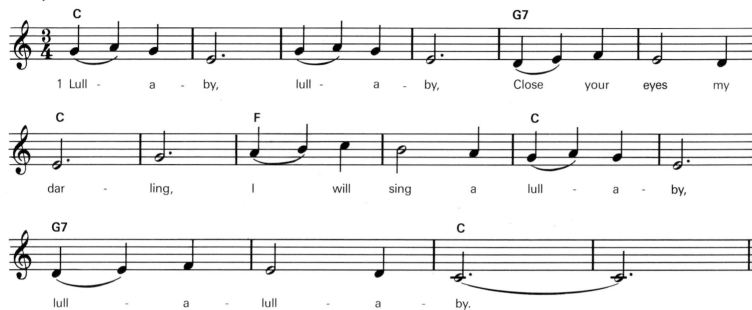

1 Lull - a - by, lull - a - by, Close your eyes my

dar - ling, I will sing a lull - a - by,

lull - a - lull - a - by.

2 Lullaby, lullaby,
Go to sleep my darling,
Listen to my lullaby,
Lull-a-lull-a-by.

3 Lullaby, lullaby,
Now you're asleep my darling,
Mm. . . . . .m
Mm. . . . . .m

Note
my darling *or*
my baby *or*
my dolly *or*
my teddy *or*
my pussy, etc.

Comments

Some children need to be encouraged to quietness and stillness. Nothing works better for them than a song such as a lullaby. As they sing encourage them to rock a baby or a teddy in their arms so they absorb the rhythm and the qualities of the song right through their bodies. See how quietly they can fade away at the end.

Follow up

Discuss with the children at what other times they must be *quiet* and *still* — when they are ill in bed and the doctor comes. Link with quiet sounds in the music corner — see Teacher's Book 1 page 19. Encourage the children to make quiet sounds and to fade away gradually as in the song.

One little brown bird

Traditional

Clearly

1 One lit - tle brown bird, Up and up he flew, A -

long came a - no - ther and that made two.

2 Two little brown birds sitting on a tree,
Along came another and that made three.

3 Three little brown birds hopping on the floor,
Along came another and that made four.

4 Four little brown birds flying round a hive,
Along came another and that made five.

5 Five little brown birds pecking at some sticks . . . . six

6 Six little brown birds flying up to heaven . . . . seven

7 Seven little brown birds sitting on a gate . . . . eight

8 Eight little brown birds perched upon a line . . . . nine

9 Nine little brown birds flew to mother hen,
Along came another and that made ten.

Comments

This is a good song for movement and can be used as a singing game with 'birds' acting in the middle. It is also an excellent example of simple rhyming words. Occasionally sing it to the children pretending to forget the last words in each line!

Circle game

Traditional tune, words by Jean Gilbert

Gaily

Pass the bean bag round and round, round and round, round and round,

Pass the bean bag round and round, Now whose turn is it?

Musical game

The children sit in a circle, one child holding the bean bag. This is passed round in one direction while everyone sings the song. Whoever is left holding the bean bag at the end of the song makes a 'sound pattern' with his/her hands/voice. Others join in. Change the instruction each time the game is played.

Variation 1

Put two instruments (e.g. drum, tambourine) into the centre of the circle. The child holding the bean bag moves to the drum and chooses a friend to play the tambourine. They have a short musical conversation. The drum leads.

Variation 2

Begin to shape the conversations. Encourage the children to echo each other e.g. drum *loud*, tambourine replies *loud*. Ask the other children what kind of sounds were being made. focus on the two basic concepts: *loud/quiet, slow/fast*.

Echo song

Words and music by Jean Gilbert

Clearly

2 We'll sing loudly, we'll sing loudly,
   We'll sing loudly, we'll sing loudly,
   This is the song we'll sing oh, this is the song we'll sing oh.

3 We'll sing quietly . . .

4 We'll sing quickly . . .

5 We'll sing slowly . . .

Comments

Start the song off yourself with the children singing the echo. Next time introduce a surprise element by altering the order of the verses. When the children know the song well perhaps some of *them* will be able to start the verses off.

Musical ideas

This song illustrates all four concepts that are being introduced at this stage. However, the children may be able to suggest other ways of singing . . . sadly, gaily, crossly, etc.

Percussion

This song can also be adapted as a finger play game:
   Clap with me . . .
   Tap with me . . .
   Wave with me . . . etc.
and a later stage it can be sung with simple percussion:
   We'll play shakers . . .
   We'll play clappers . . .
   We'll play tambourines . . .
If there are not enough instruments to go round, the echo can be mimed.

Contents 1B

Note to the teacher

By this stage, most children are ready to join in more formal, corporate ways of singing. The songs suggested for Stage 1B encourage this development in a number of ways:

a) The melodic range of most songs is extended.

b) Simple ideas for accompaniment have been suggested.

For further ideas and information on singing see *General Notes*.

Most of the songs illustrate some of the concepts and ideas suggested in the 'sounds' sections and more detailed comments can be found with each song. These should be discussed and the appropriate interpretation encouraged. 'Listen, listen' is basically a quieter song; 'I'm a great big lorry' and 'The land of the monsters' make use of dynamics and tempo.

Some useful songs

The following songs underline the musical ideas that are introduced in Stage 1B. They can all be found in the recommended songbooks.

Loud/Quiet

Kum ba yah (someone's singing/laughing/dancing/praying/sleeping, etc. Interpret each verse according to the words you choose.)
Traditional West Indian

Vary the singing of your songs to suit the words and the mood. Ask your children which way *they* think the songs should be sung.

Fast/Slow

The snail (slow finishing quickly on the last verse)   *Sing-a-Song-One*
Train is a-coming (speed of the singing can represent the speed of the train)   *Apusskidu, Sing-a-Song One*
The princess (interpret each verse to accompany the *movement* of the children)   *Sing-a-Song One, This Little Puffin, Okki-tokki-unga*

High/Low

The little red bus (high and low on the sound words in the chorus)   *Sing-a-Song Two*
Six little frogs ('frogs jump high, frogs jump low' in the chorus — this is also an echo song)   *Knock at the Door*
Brown girl in the ring (Plum, plum, plum — low, high, high)   *Knock at the Door*

Long Short

Somebody's knocking at your door (ask the children to tell you on which word the *long* note comes)   *Knock at the Door*

Twinkle, twinkle little star,   The North Wind doth blow (note that the long
    notes come on the rhyming words)   *Knock at the Door*
I went to visit a farm one day (the long notes come on the animal
    noises)   *Sing-a-Song One*

When pointing out long notes in a song, remember to *sing* them as long notes.
They will also contrast with the others which are *shorter*.

Although song examples have been given for *high/low* and *long/short* it is
better at this stage to concentrate on environmental sounds that illustrate these
concepts, and to point out in passing parallels in the songs the children sing.

Use of notation

Some phrases and patterns from the songs have been notated in the Pupils'
Book. These are intended simply as a visual introduction to written music
although one or two practical suggestions about using these phrases can be
developed once the songs have been thoroughly learned. In Stage 2 the
complete song melody is notated.

With the class

Take one of the phrases from the Pupils' Book and tap out the rhythm on a wood
block or drum, e.g.

What kind   of shoes   shall   we   put   on   to - day?

Ask the children which words from a song they know fit with this pattern.

Play a melodic phrase.

Ask the children to sing the phrase to 'la'. Then ask them to identify the song.
Not all the phrases used are the beginnings of the songs.

In the music corner

Copy out one or two phrases on to individual workcards. Make the necessary
chime bars available and let the children play these. This is intended as an aural
activity and not really a 'music reading' exercise. Notes for accompaniments and
percussion work ideas can be found with each song.

Put on your shoes

Words and music by Leonora Davies

Rhythmically

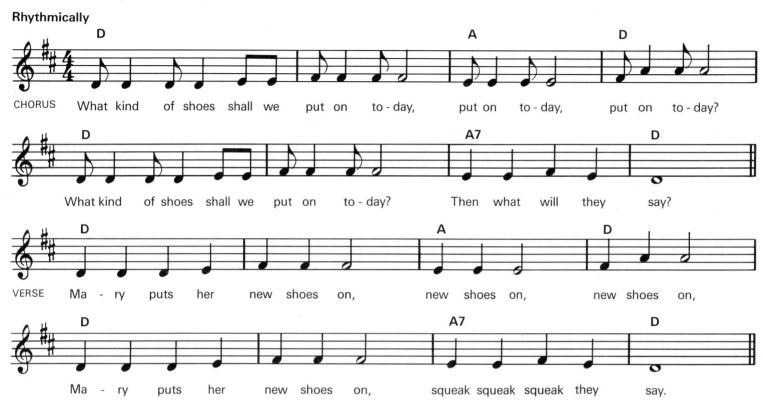

CHORUS What kind of shoes shall we put on to-day, put on to-day, put on to-day?

What kind of shoes shall we put on to-day? Then what will they say?

VERSE Ma – ry puts her new shoes on, new shoes on, new shoes on,

Ma – ry puts her new shoes on, squeak squeak squeak they say.

Comments

5   This song links with page 10 of Pupils' Book 1B. See Activity Sheet 5.

Musical ideas and percussion

Different shoes can make *loud* or *quiet* sounds and people walk *quickly* or *slowly*. One or two children (not too many) can play throughout:

Mary puts her new shoes on   (sandpaper block or scraped cymbal)

Singing game

The children hold hands and dance round in a circle as they sing the question 'What kind of shoes shall we put on to-day?' The teacher then asks Mary to choose what kind of shoes to sing about. Mary describes the shoes, possibly the ones she is already wearing, and then walks round in the middle while everyone else stands still and sings the verse.

   This could also be played in a sitting circle where a 'shoe' is passed round as the children sing. Pictures of various shoes are face down in a pile in the middle. The child holding the shoe at the end of the chorus chooses a card which provides the basis for the next verse.

26

Music box

Words and music by Leonora Davies

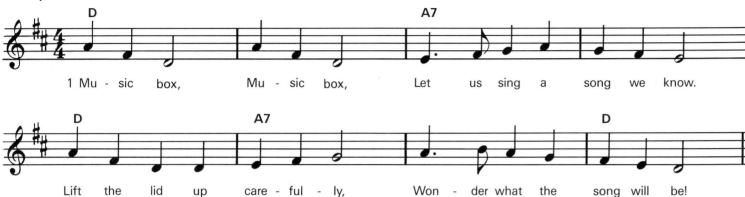

Clearly

1 Mu - sic box, Mu - sic box, Let us sing a song we know.

Lift the lid up care - ful - ly, Won - der what the song will be!

2 Music box, Music box,
Let us play our instruments.
Lift the lid up carefully,
Wonder what the sound will be!

Comments

This activity can be freely adapted by teachers to suit their own groups of children. It provides an opportunity for the children to make individual responses and to develop the musical ideas already introduced to them, in their own way.

Musical games

1 Place the titles or the children's drawings of familiar songs into the 'Music box'. The children sit round in a circle.
Everyone sings verse 1 of the Music box song while an 'apple' is passed round. Whoever has the 'apple' on the word 'be' may have a turn.
The child takes a song title or drawing out of the box and must choose how he/she wishes the song to be sung — loud or quiet, fast or slow.
The class sings. They can then discuss whether they liked the song sung that way. Would another choice have been 'better' perhaps?

2 Place an instrument in front of each child in the circle and a representative selection inside the box.
Sing verse 2 and pass the 'apple' round as before.
The child whose turn it is chooses an instrument from the box and decides how he/she will play.
All those with similar instruments can join in following the playing of the leader.

3 The game could be further structured by encouraging the leader to play a set rhythmic pattern. This could be very simple, for example:

tap, tap, tap, rest (clappers)
or shake, tap, shake, tap (shakers)

6 and 7 This game will be more successful if the children have already played some clapping or echo games (Teacher's Book 1 page 15).
Link with page 14 of Pupil's Book 1B and structure the music corner to encourage 'echo' playing.

A colourful music box could be made from a cardboard carton decorated with illustrations of familiar songs or pictures of musical instruments.

Round and round the classroom

Traditional tune, words by Leonora Davies

Not too fast

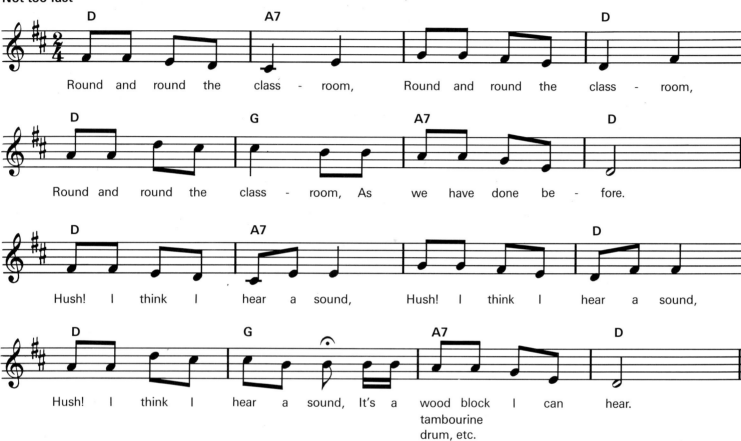

Round and round the class - room, Round and round the class - room,

Round and round the class - room, As we have done be - fore.

Hush! I think I hear a sound, Hush! I think I hear a sound,

Hush! I think I hear a sound, It's a wood block I can hear.
tambourine
drum, etc.

Comments

This is another adaptation of a traditional melody. The musical game incorporates the use of percussion instruments so that teachers who are a little apprehensive about their use can give their children the opportunity of using them within a controlled framework.

Musical game

This is in fact a variation of the listening game described on page 10 of Teacher's Book 1.
Teachers may prefer to start with a sitting down version of the game:

Sitting in the classroom,
Sitting in the classroom,
Sitting in the classroom,
Upon the yellow mat.

Hush! I think I hear a sound,
Hush! I think I hear a sound,
Hush! I think I hear a sound.

A child hidden behind a screen or bookcase with a number of *familiar* instruments now chooses one and plays it. The children in the circle guess which instrument is playing and sing the last line:

'It's a wood block I can hear'.

The game continues with someone else behind the screen.
Select instruments with distinctive sounds to begin with such as a drum, shaker and clappers. Later make it more complex by using groups of instruments which sound the same:

those making short sounds (wood block, tambour, clappers)
those making long sounds (triangle, finger cymbals, chime bar)

Further development

1   The children march round the classroom singing the printed version of the song. Three or four children hide behind the screen. They choose one of them to play an instrument while the marching children stop and sing 'Hush! I think I hear a sound'.

2   The teacher plays a steady beat on a drum or tambour as the children march and continues to play while the new sound is introduced from behind the screen. (Children find it quite difficult to discriminate when two sounds are played together.)

3   For an occasional 'teaser' two/three sounds can be played together.

I'm a great big lorry

Traditional tune, words by Leonora Davies

1 I'm a great big lor - ry, Go - ing ve - ry slow - ly,

Bet - ter slow down, The lights are red.

2 I'm a busy police car,
  Travelling very quickly,
  Listen to my siren,
  Don't get in my way.

3 I'm a big red bus,
  Taking people home.
  Ring my bell,
  It's time to stop.

Musical ideas

This song incorporates not only the contrasts of *fast* and *slow* but also change of speed, that of *getting slower*. The variation and change of speed can be reflected in the singing.

When everyone has sung all the verses, divide the children into three groups: a slow one for the lorry, a fast one for the police car and an average one for the big red bus. Change them over so that they all have a turn at singing each verse. Children playing an ostinato will need to control the speed of their playing to support each verse.

Movement

This song should be acted out in the hall. Different approaches could be used:

Use a tambour to control the speed as all the children move together. Keep varying the speed and include several stops.

Divide the children into three groups and use a different sound for each group: a tambour, triangle and wood block, for instance. Let them move separately at first, then with the help of an older child or adult play for two groups to move at once. This will require very careful listening and body control from everyone.

Occasionally improvise streets, traffic lights and bus stops, using ropes and hoops, etc.. Agree upon a sound signal for the traffic lights and appoint one or two 'policemen' to control crossings.

Ostinato

The following repeating tune can be played on any tuned instrument:

Try a different instrument for each verse. Ask the children which one they would choose. It could be:

I'm a great big lorry — alto or bass xylophone
I'm a busy police car — glockenspiel
I'm a big red bus — chime bars

Listen, listen

Words and music by Leonora Davies

Quietly

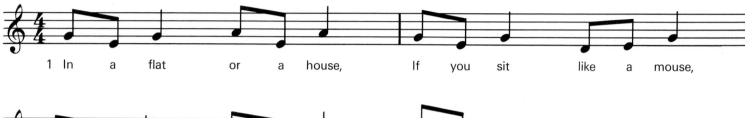

1 In a flat or a house, If you sit like a mouse,

There are sounds to be heard, If you lis - ten, lis - ten.

2 Tabby cat is purring now,
Hear the kettle's whistle go.
There are sounds to be heard,
If you listen, listen.

Comments

This song incorporates some of the listening ideas from Pupils' Book 1A pages 2 and 3 and reintroduces the idea of grouping sounds. Ask the children to think of other *domestic sounds* and to make up some more verses. Tape record some sounds from home for the children to identify. Encourage them to do the same. These sounds can now be sorted according to the concepts already introduced and the children can be more specific in their analysis. Which sounds are *quiet* and *long*, which ones are *loud* and *short* and so on.

Musical ideas

10 These groups of sounds can now be sorted into different categories according to the concepts introduced in the first six pages of Pupils' Book 1B. See Activity Sheet 10.

Music corner

Link with sorting activities, see Teacher's Book 1 page 18.

Ostinato

This simple repeating tune used as an accompaniment can provide extra interest:

Counting song

Words and music by Wendy Van Blankenstein

Brightly

VERSE
1 I can see cher - ries high up in the tree,

And there's a black - bird, he's sing - ing to me.

Come let's eat cher - ries, One, two, three, four,

Shake the tree, Shake the tree, I'd like some more.

CHORUS One, two, three, four, five, six, seven, eight, nine, ten.

One, two, three, four, five, six, seven, eight, nine, ten.

2 Let's collect conkers all shiny and brown,
   Look for the prickles that fall to the ground,
   Scuff the leaves over so crispy and gold,
   Then pick up the conkers they're lovely to hold.
   CHORUS

3 Can I have sixpence to go the the shops?
   One, two, three, four, five, six pennies I've got,
   But sixpence in pennies doesn't last long,
   Six, five, four, three, two, one, now they're all gone.
   CHORUS

Comments

Use the first verse to begin with and make up other verses for all the fruit trees that your children know. This then becomes a very useful song for Autumn and for Harvest Festival. Add percussion as suggested.

Introduce the second and third verses later. Older children will enjoy these.

Singing game

(for the 'fruit tree' verses)
Stand in a circle with one child in the centre as the tree. Sing and mime the verses. Sing and skip round in the chorus. Choose a new 'tree' for each verse.

Percussion

Shakers	'Shake the tree, shake the tree . . .'
Bird whistle (or a child)	'And there's a blackbird, he's singing to me',
Clappers	Play throughout the counting chorus.

Guitar is easier in D. Capo up 3 frets.

Low and high

Words and music by Jean Gilbert

Clearly

(1) Lis-ten to the big chime, dong, dong, dong, We must sing down ve-ry low for his song.

(2) Lis-ten to the lit-tle chime, ting, ting, ting, We must go up ve-ry high as we sing.

Musical ideas

Introduce this song when you are building the concepts of *high* and *low*. These musical concepts are often difficult for young children to grasp; help them by placing the top C chime bar on a brick or tall carton so that they can link with the *visual* concept of high. Refer back to pages 5 and 6 of the Pupils' Book 1B and the cassette.

Further verses can include other high and low sounds:
Listen to the big dog, woof, woof, woof,
We must sing down very low for his song.
Listen to the little puppy, yap, yap, yap,
We must go up very high as we sing.

This song is very easy to sing as a *round*. Get a grown up or an older child to help for the first time. The second part starts when the first part reaches the line, 'Listen to the little chime'.

Further links

Go on a 'high and low' walk. Listen out for high and low sounds. Look for high and low objects. See also *The music corner* (Teacher's Book 1 page 31), and *Three little piggies* page 43.

Pussy willow

Traditional song

Quietly

I know a lit - tle pus - sy, Her coat is sil - ver grey. She

lives down in the mead - ow not ver - y far a - way. Al -

- though she is a pus - sy, She'll nev - er be a cat, For

she's a pus - sy wil - low, Now what d'you think of that? - Meow,

meow, meow, meow, meow, meow, meow, meow, SCAT!

This song helps to build the concepts of *going up* and *coming down*. The tune goes up step by step from the bottom to the top of the musical ladder or scale, then comes down on all the 'meows' and jumps back up again on the 'SCAT'.

When the children know the song well let them act it by starting in a crouched position, rising gradually, then coming down quickly on the meows with a big jump on 'SCAT'.

Sounds

Words by Julie Holder. Music by Paul Reade adapted by Jean Gilbert

At a steady pace

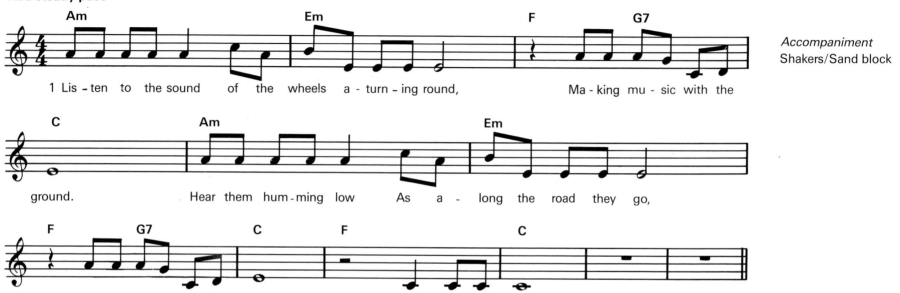

Accompaniment
Shakers/Sand block

1 Lis - ten to the sound of the wheels a - turn - ing round, Ma - king mu - sic with the

ground. Hear them hum - ming low As a - long the road they go,

Making mu - sic with the ground. Wheels turn - ing round.

2   Wheels a-turning round
    Through the puddles on the ground,
    It's a wet and muddy sound.
    Hear the wheels hiss
    As along the road they swish,
    It's a wet and muddy sound,

Suggested percussion
cymbals played
with a wire brush

3   Listen to the sound
    Of the wheels a-turning round,
    Printing patterns as they wind.
    Watch the wheels go by
    As along the road they fly,
    Printing patterns you can find,
    Wheels turning round.

a pattern played
on a tambour or drum

Comments

Sing this song very steadily throughout to underline the feel of a basic *pulse* or *beat*.

If you live near a busy highway make a recording of the sound of a steady flow of traffic. Compare it with a recording made on a rainy day.

The jumping song

Words by Michael Sullivan. Music by Chris Adams

Jolly

2   Here comes Jack in the Box — JUMP!
    Jumping Jack in the Box — JUMP!
    Lift the lid and then
    Up he jumps again,
    Jumping Jack in the Box — JUMP!

3   Here comes Ferdinand Frog — JUMP!
    Jumping Ferdinand Frog — JUMP!
    Jumping in the night
    When the moon is bright,
    Jump with Ferdinand Frog — JUMP!

4   Here comes Sue Kangaroo — JUMP!
    Jumping Sue Kangaroo — JUMP!
    She can jump all day,
    You can jump this way,
    Jump with Sue Kangaroo — JUMP!

Musical ideas

This is a lovely example of a tune jumping up — actually on the word 'Jump!'
Can the children play any two notes on a tuned instrument to make a 'jumping up' pattern?

Land of the monsters

Words and music by Jean Gilbert

Dramatically

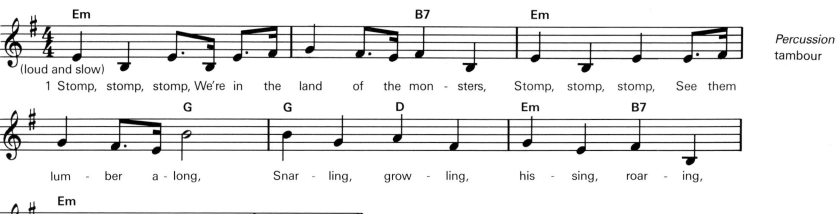

Percussion
tambour

1 Stomp, stomp, stomp, We're in the land of the mon - sters, Stomp, stomp, stomp, See them

lum - ber a - long, Snar - ling, grow - ling, his - sing, roar - ing,

List - en to our mon - ster song. _____

Suggested percussion

2 Creep, creep, creep,
This monster goes very slowly,
Creep, creep, creep,
See him steal along,
Looking, listening, stopping, watching,
Listen to our monster song.

(quiet and slow)

tambourine played very quietly

3 Run, run, run,
This monster goes very quickly,
Run, run, run,
See him race along,
Quick as lightning, quiet as grey cloud,
Listen to our monster song.

(quiet and fast)

clappers or tapped triangle

4 Roar, roar, roar,
This monster goes very quickly,
Roar, roar, roar,
See him thunder along,
Lashing, crashing, twisting, turning,
Listen to our monster song.

(loud and fast)

drum played with a padded
beater

Movement

Let all of the children portray each of the monsters and accompany their movement with the percussion instruments you have used with the song. You could then, in the next hall session, work in four groups choosing two or three children to accompany each group. Let each group perform on its own and then perhaps two at a time. The dancers freeze into a monster statue when their music stops.

Further dramatic movement can be based on the idea that the children have gone back in time to the land of the monsters, and that, from their time machine, they can observe each monster — how it moves, what it eats, how it behaves. The *Listen, Move and Dance* record (moving percussion and electronic sound pictures — HMVCLP 3531) has some suitable extracts to accompany this movement.

Musical ideas

11 The concepts *loud/quiet* and *fast/slow* are linked together in pairs to describe each monster. See Activity Sheet 11.

The toy cupboard

Words and music by Jean Gilbert

Brightly

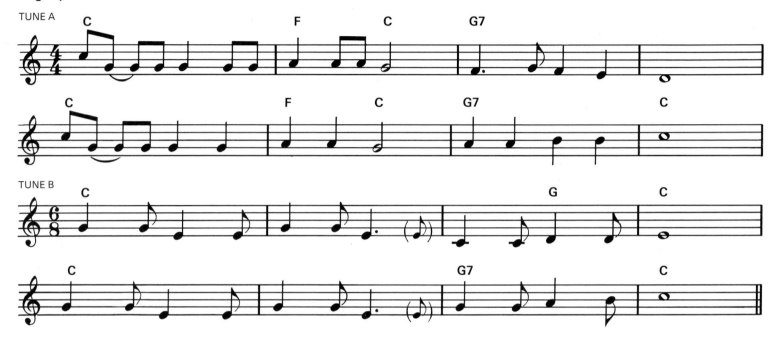

1   Open the toy cupboard — out with the toys,
(A) Tumbling on the ground,
    Ready for all the girls and boys,
    See what we have found.

2   Wind up the racing car — put it down
(A) Watch it zoom away . . .
    Turn it round and race it back,
    It will go all day.

3   Teddy bear is lying there,
(B) Flat upon his nose,
    He's a slow and clumsy bear
    Just see the way he goes.

4   Play the drum and blow the pipe
(B) And shake the tambourine,
    What a noise for all the soldiers,
    Soldiers of the Queen.

5   Here's the little baby doll
(B) Lying in her bed,
    See her eyes that open and shut,
    See her curly head.   (quiet)

6   Open the toy cupboard — back with the toys,
(A) Clear them all away,
    Tidy the shelves and shut the door,
    What a lovely play!

Musical ideas

12 The four toys relate to four different concepts: racing car (*fast*), teddy (*slow*), soldiers (*loud*), doll (*quiet*). The song uses two contrasting tunes; which one would the children choose for each toy? Ask them which toy is the quiet one, which one the fast one and so on; then see if they can suggest suitable percussion to accompany each verse.

Make up some more verses with the children about their favourite toys and ask them to choose the most suitable tune.

Movement

This song is a good one for dramatic movement. It could also be turned into a little musical play.

Look at the fish

Words and music by Leonora Davies.

This song encourages individual children to respond by singing their own names and a short phrase. It could be introduced alongside other activities to do with names or linked with a topic on fish or water.

Movement

When Mary has sung her response she can be invited out in front or in the middle of the singing circle to 'swim' round in the sea.

Suggested percussion

A group of children can choose suitable instruments (glockenspiel, chime bars, xylophone, shakers, bells) to accompany the movement. Extend the idea in the hall. Half the children could play while the other half do the movement. Encourage variety in the playing by introducing the concepts of *loud/quiet* and *fast/slow*; instruments could play on their own or in small groups of two and three. The children moving must listen as they dance and reflect the quality of the music in their movement.

What can we hear coming down the street?

Traditional tune, words by Leonora Davies

Brightly

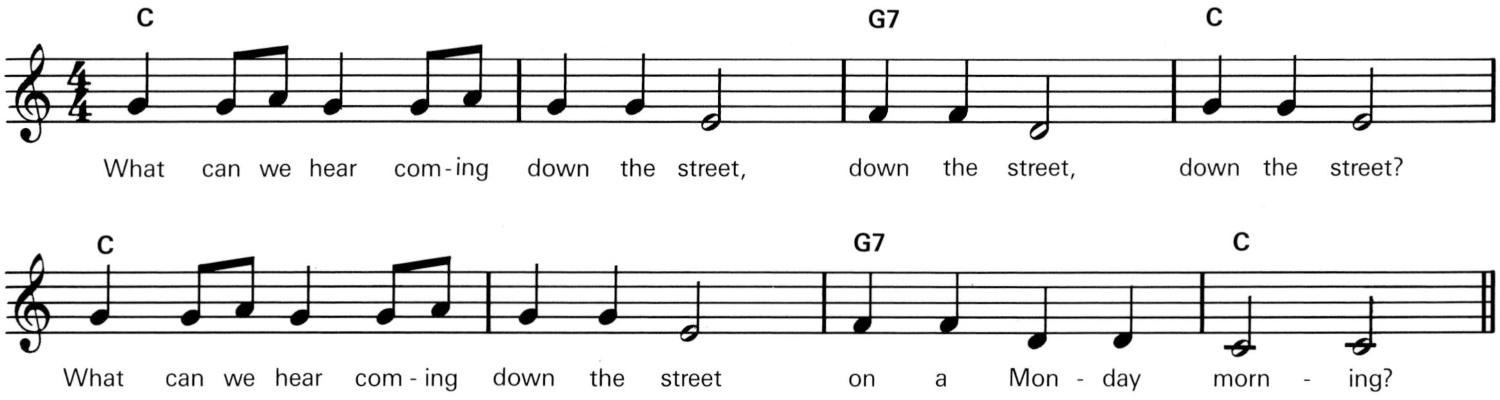

Singing game

The children sit in a circle. They have already made picture cards of all the different things they can see and hear in the street. Put these in a hat and pass this round the circle as everyone sings. The child holding the hat at the end of the song takes a card and imitates the sound suggested by the drawing. Everyone joins in. Related activities are described in Teacher's Book 1 page 28.

Follow my leader

English folk song

Brightly

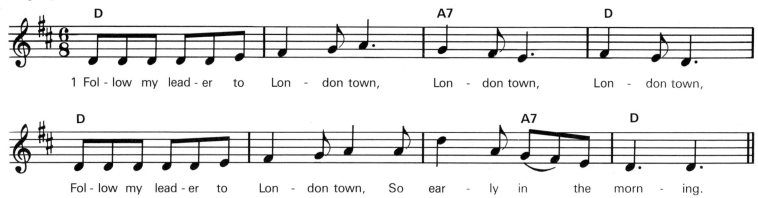

1 Fol - low my lead - er to Lon - don town, Lon - don town, Lon - don town,

Fol - low my lead - er to Lon - don town, So ear - ly in the morn - ing.

2 Marching around in London town,
London town, London town,
Marching around in London town,
So early in the morning.

3 Dancing around . . .

4 Creeping around . . .

5 Skipping around . . .

6 Playing our rhythms . . .

Musical ideas

The tune in this song *goes up* and *comes down* in each half. Show the children the shape, moving your hands up and down as you sing and ask the children to do the same. See if they can do it by themselves afterwards. Draw the shape and ask individual children to trace it as they sing.

Each verse can be sung at a *different speed* and with *different dynamics*:
    Marching — at a steady pace and sung firmly
    Dancing — freely and sung lightly
    Creeping — slowly and quietly
    Skipping — at a skipping pace and sung brightly

Singing game

Play as a 'follow my leader' game. Sing verse 1 as a chorus and during the singing choose a new leader for the next verse. Encourage the children to find different ways of moving on which to base further verses.

Percussion

Accompany with a different instrument for each verse:

Marching — drum

Dancing — bells   freely

Creeping — shakers

Skipping — tambourine

Three little piggies

Words and music by Guy Carawan

Not too fast

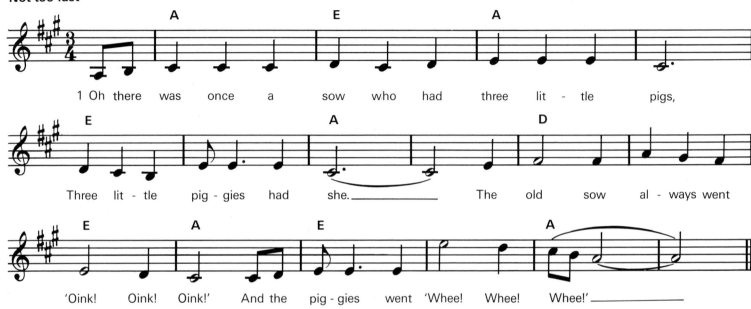

1 Oh there was once a sow who had three lit - tle pigs,

Three lit - tle pig - gies had she. The old sow al - ways went

'Oink! Oink! Oink!' And the pig - gies went 'Whee! Whee! Whee!'

2 Now, one day, one of those three little pigs,
To the other two piggies said he:
'Why don't we try to go 'Oink! Oink! Oink!'
Instead of going 'Whee! Whee! Whee!'?'

3 Now those three little piggies grew skinny and lean,
Skinny they well might be.
For they always tried to go 'Oink! Oink! Oink!'
Instead of going 'Whee! Whee! Whee!'

4 Now those three little piggies, they up and they died,
A very sad sight to see.
So don't ever try to go 'Oink! Oink! Oink!'
When you ought to go 'Whee! Whee! Whee!'

Musical ideas

This is an excellent illustration to use when talking about *high* and *low* voices.
Link with the work on *The Three Bears* (See Teacher's Book 1 page 31) and
with Pupils' Book 1B page 15.

Divide the children into two groups for the 'Oinks' and 'Whees'. Be sure to
change over so that they all have the experience of singing the different pitches.

Carra barra wirra canna

Words and music by Morva Cogan

Andante

1 There's a lake in South Aus - tra - lia, lit - tle lake with love - ly name,

And the sto - ry wo - ven round it, from the lit - tle chil - dren came.

Ev - 'ry night you hear the mo - thers croon this love - ly lul - la - by,

Croon a - cross the moon - lit wa - ters, to the star up in the sky.

Car - ra bar - ra wir - ra can - na, lit - tle star up - on the lake,

Guide me through the hours of dark - ness, keep me safe - ly till I wake.

2 Little children's heads are nodding, drowsy crooning fills the air,
Little eyes at last are closing, and the boat of dreams is there.
Guide my boat across the waters, cross the waters still and deep,
Light me with your little candle, safely to the land of sleep.
Carra barra wirra canna, little star upon the lake,
Guide me through the hours of darkness, keep me safely till I wake.

The story referred to in the first verse is one of many from the aboriginal tribes of Australia. It tells of a lake, which in the Boat of Dreams the children of the tribes crossed each night to the Land of Sleep on the other side.

When a wicked Whowie tried to drown them the moon came to the rescue and sent a star down to guide the boat. Then the wicked Whowie tried to drown the star but the moon was watching and threw the wicked Whowie up into the Milky Way. It is doomed to stay up in the sky for ever and ever.

Now it is safe for all children to go across the magic lake every night to the Land of Sleep, guided by the little star (*carra barra wirra canna*, which means 'Little star upon the lake').

Sing this lovely song very clearly and quietly. The chorus can be accompanied by a single triangle played at the beginning of alternate bars:

Chorus

Movement

Slow controlled rowing movements during the chorus.

Platypus song

Words and music by Morva Cogan

Steadily

O rid - dle, rid - dle, rid - dle me, A pla - ty - pus I be! And

ne - ver was there e - ver such a mixed up bloke as me! I've a

brown fur coat like a cat And a tail that's ve - ry flat, With a

bill like lea-ther I'm a ve-ry fun-ny fel-ler And I can't say fair-er than that! I

like to get up in the morn-ing when the sun is shin-ing bright, Then I

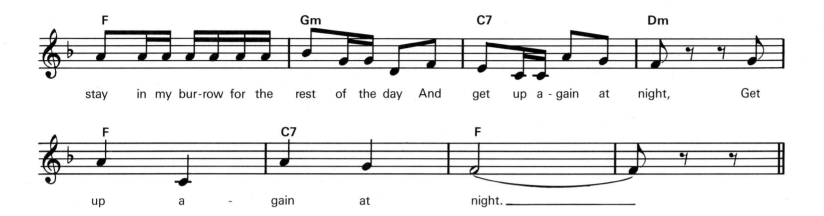

stay in my bur-row for the rest of the day And get up a-gain at night, Get

up a - gain at night.

This attractive Australian children's song spells out the odd physical make up of the platypus in the form of a riddle; thus it is a good song to include in any project about animals or Australia. The melody could also help the children to make up riddles about other animals:

O riddle, riddle, riddle me,
Can you guess what I must be?
And never was there ever such
A mixed up bloke as me!

I've a . . .
And a . . .
With a . . .
And I can't say fairer than that!

I like to . . .
Then I . . . .
Can you guess what I must be?
Can you guess what I must be?

Who's that tapping at the window?

Words and music by Wendy Van Blankenstein

Cheekily

Who's that tap-ping at the win-dow? Who's that knock-ing at the door?

Who's that tap-ping at the win-dow? I've heard that be - fore!

ANSWER

It's Joe tapping at the window,
It's Joe knocking at the door,
It's Joe tapping at the window,
He's done that before!

Musical ideas

This song focuses on *quiet* tapping and *loud* knocking sounds. Underline the contrast by using two different body sounds for these like tapping with two fingers on the palm of the hand and slapping thighs.

The song is also patterned on the *question* and *answer* form. This provides a good opportunity for dividing the children into two groups for singing.

Singing game

The children sit in a circle to sing the verse and play the rhythms. When Joe hears his name called he goes into the middle to do the actions while everyone sings the answer. The game continues with someone else in the middle.

Percussion

Add variety to the game by introducing two distinctive sounds like clappers for the tapping (played quietly) and a drum for the knocking.

Ostinato

The following simple repeating pattern can provide further activity if needed: